Turning Heads
GOD FOR

In marketplace

By Norma Brown

TURNING HEADS
FOR GOD
IN MARKETPLACE

Written by Norma Brown
Mcdonough, Georgia

*The Lord doesn't see things the way
you see them.
People judge by outward appearance, but the
Lord looks at the heart."
1 Samuel 16:7 (NLT*

Acknowledgements

I THANK GOD FOR HIS HOLY SPIRIT TO WRITE THIS BOOK AND SHARE HIS GLORY WITH ALL. HE HAS SUBSTAINED ME..

TO MY LOVING, PATIENCE HUSBAND CHARLES BROWN

You have given me himself in so many ways, thank you. I love you and thank God for you.

THANKS TO MY LOVING MOM ANDREA BERRY

Without all your love through all the years and your true joy, and heart for the things for God Thanks for your Prayers and thanks for being the best mom ever. YOU ARE A EXAMPLE OF THE GRACE OF GOD LOVE YOU MUCH

TO SERENA BROWN THE MOST WONDERFUL DAUGHTER

With you in my life you have blessed me to be the mom I am and may God continue to use you in others life as a true blessing.

THANK YOU MINISTER DEBBIE GREEN

You are a God-send who has opened up a chapter of amazing possibilities for me and my family through the rough times with your prayer. Your faithfulness is wonderful! God bless you and your family.

TO MY LOVING PASTOR AND FIRST LADY ANDRE,KIM LANDERS

To my loving Pastor André Landers and wife, First Lady Kim Landers, thank you for showing that following God is the way of true joy. You have been an example to many and your lifestyle and dedication to God and his word .Your teaching has made my life a blessing. To the Higher Living Community Team and Prayer Team Thank you for your relentless dedication to empower others with what God grace that he has given you. I am so grateful to you God Bless

A SPECIAL THANKS TO ALL THE COUNSELORS AT THE COMMUNITY IMPACT CENTER

Without you and your teaching and love I would not be writing this book when I first joined the church I was told to attend your classes by one of your teachers and thank you Beverly Cole for teaching me. You were directed by God for me in my trouble time thank you so much God Bless.

TO MY ONLY LOVING BROTHERS AND SISTERS I GREW UP WITH I LOVE YOU NORMAN BERRY, ANGELA BERRY, KURT GARNER

I thank God for what He has placed in us, and I thank you for sharing my youth with me and our adulthood May God continue to keep us together. .

A SPECIAL LAST BUT NOT LEAST THANKS TO MARY SCOTT

Thank you for being there for me in those rough years when I was trying to find my way through school. God has truly sent me a angel love you and bless you and your family. You were an inspiration and I love you.

Table of Contents

FORWARD

CHRISTIAN COUNSELOR NORMA BROWN

We are the salt of the World
You make the world a better place. (Mark 9:50)

In "Turning Heads for God," Norma leads the reader on a journey to understand how to gain true success, identity and joy. She gives you a personal look at her own journey to purpose and fulfillment. This is an excellent tool to help you to refocus and revalue all areas of your life. It is never too late to get it right.

Although my mother raised us alone, I had a typical upbringing with my brothers and sisters. My father was not around, but he loved us. As a child, I got into mischief and lived to regret the bad choices. Thank be to god that he chastise those he love. Hebrew 12:6

One mistake changed my life: This began my journey to make up for all my wrong actions and to prove that I was not a failure. However, God saw different. If you are reading this book and you are at a crossroad in your life then it is not over, If you are reading this book and drama is in your life it is not over, If you are reading this book and rejection is in your life it is not over. Just like the awesome God saw me through my broken-ness he can see you through too. He loves you and he is not like man. He has no favorites in his people and what he did for me he also can do for you. Colossians 3:-25

THANK YOU FOR ALLOWING ME TO TAKE THIS JOURNEY WITH YOU .GOD BLESS.

FINAL WORD

With God All Things Are Possible!

THE CALL OF THE MENTOR

The one who plants is no greater than the one who waters: because both are needed to make the growth process complete. A spiritual increase cannot come unless both of these principles are at work-because they both represent true mentorship. A mentor can be either a plant or water in the life of a profit in the making. His or her role must be discerned. Those whom God entrust to mentor must truly understand what their purpose is in helping others to fulfill their destiny. As a planter the job of plowing through hard and unbroken ground in the heart of the protégé. Love is watering that drives the son or daughter into a deeper spiritual development. In these last days true mentors are vitally needed.

A GENERATION IS WAITING TO RISE INTO DESTINY!

To schedule a speaking engagement, or receive information about teaching material or products by Christian Counselor Norma Brown please contact 678-592-2972

COMPLETE BY DESIGN
WWW.COMPLETEBYDESIGN.ORG
P.O BOX 567
MCDONOUGH GA.30252

1

THE GIFT AND
THE JOURNEY

There is one thing most everyone can agree upon: we all want peace, love and security. That's what I wanted when I started my journey to be successful.

I grew up as a normal child with a loving mom and dad. My family believed in moral living and treating people right, and I thank my mom for that. My mother later raised us as a single parent and we never missed love or support and as kids we were loved . We Laughed and played as brother and sisters . All normal things kids would do.. We were content and secure in our home. . At a young age I loved styling my dolls hair, I notice that I like doing hair more that playing with the dolls .I would cry if I could not put real hair products on their hair. I came up with another idea, Later was I to find out this was the creative business owner being developed. I would think of other strategies. I would wait till I get to school and do my friends hair. Wow for some strange reason they let me do whatever I wanted to do to their hair, they would actually wait on me in the High school restroom to get their hair styled. Man did this raise my confidence. I thought I can start charging a fee, and guess what it worked. This brief journey on the path I was about to travel had many trials I was yet to understand or handle. As a teen we come across a decision that will alter your life instantly. This life altering decision was when I thought to be accepted was to be popular and being at the wrong place cause me to be raped by a peer that was 5 years older than myself. Confused on what happened shame and guilt over took me. I later found out I was Pregnant, which I begged my mom not to let me keep and so I didn't. I decided I have to pick up where I left off and decided to go to Attend Cosmetology school and not think about what happen to me. One thing I notice that I had a hard time being productive with family, don't get me wrong I love them but something wasn't genuine like it once was and it affected my emotions finances and health. Thank God He had a plan (He said He will never leave you or forsake you) I met My wonderful Husband so opposite of me . Everything looked promising. Although my marriage had some ups and downs, we were hanging in there and life seemed great. One night

I will never forget, I decided to go to church to listen to a speaker. The speaker was a dynamic man of God. I know this because my heart was pounding the entire time I was listening to him. I knew this was the Holy Spirit.

The speaker talked about "covenant soul ties" and how they can hinder us from moving forward. He discussed how we connect ourselves to spirits that are not in God's will. Numbers 14:24 He asked us to recall our first sexual encounter and asked everyone to stand up who had sex outside of marriage. The entire church stood up!

After everyone was standing, he prayed for every that had a soul covenant that wasn't godly and that connected itself to us and we repeated the prayer that it was sin and repented in the name of Jesus. At the very moment, I felt a release of peace come over me. Then he told us to confess the shameful thing we had never told anyone to someone we trusted. Little did I know that this was my testimony By the Blood of the lamb and word of my testimony. From this, I learned that to be "people free" you have to be open to confess what Jesus delivered you from, which is your testimony. This was also the beginning of my call to be a priest and to carry this message to the workplace. Romans 6:22 *Now you have been set free from sin, having become slaves of God you have your fruit to holiness and the end, everlasting life.*

Foundation

The beginning of knowledge is from God. –
Prov. 1:17

Our source is God... God says I knew you before you were formed in your mother womb. *Before you were born, I knew you, and know the plans I have for you plans of good and not of evil to prosper you and show you an expected end.* Jeremiah 1:5

It is great to know that before we were born, God knew us and had a plan. No matter what your family did or did not do, you have a call and a mandate on your life, and it is so much better than our desire. Don't get me wrong, God rains on the just and the unjust, so our lives still have problems, but the important message here is that greatness is in you.

The message of my book is primarily for people who have great gifts inside them and how to honor God with them . The truth is, God has given you a gift which he will make room for. We are not called to copy another but we are cre-ated for Gods pleasure Psalms 35:27 everyone is called to purpose. Jesus said, follow me and I will make you a disciple John 13:35. A disciple is not above his teacher, or a servant above his master.

Our main purpose therefore is to follow Christ. Our life starts with following Jesus not man, not your husband, not your boss not your friends. True success is eternal.

It's time to look within.

The root of righteous yield fruit which is sown in peace – James 3:18

No More Selfishness

Since we did not create ourselves, and our creator is God and God is love, when we follow the roadmap God has ordained or us, we will leave a mark in lives that will never be erased. It's not about us and our accomplishments; it's about what Jesus did for us on the cross. Our Lord came to the earth so that we could have life and have it more abundantly. We are already blessed to be a blessing. Colossians 1:20

Ambitious Leaders

I was so ambitious and determined to succeed in business that I read every book and went to every class to get better at my craft. I became smarter, but not wiser. I was still working paycheck to paycheck because I still did not understand the purpose of success and wealth.

During that time, I learned that God's ways are higher than our ways. He not only has a purpose for us individually, has a purpose for our jobs and our marriages. 1 Corinthians 12:13.

Starting with Adam fallen man has sinned and walked away from his relationship with God in order to go his own way. Genesis 3:17 Until you come to the end of yourself and allow Gods grace to guide your life, you will never have true wealth. God wants to lead you in every area of your life. When we allow God this privilege, we are ready to become great Godly leaders.

Selfless- vs. Selfish

In John 3:16, For God so loved the world He gave His only begotten son so that whoever believes in Him will be saved. This is the beginning of true life. God sacrificed His most prized possession for mans sin just to have a relationship with his creation. God sowed his son and it was the ultimate selfless act.

Because we are created in God's image, we are capable of great sacrifice and selfless acts. We are also called to sow in order to reap rewards. When God "sowed Jesus," He reaped the salvation of the world. What sacrifice are your willing to sow to reap the benefits of success?

Success

The spirit of fear keeps many people from achieving true success. Because of fear, many waste much time concerned about their looks, their status in life and even who will look after them in their old age. Many people are also carrying old wombs of rejection and being told that they are failures, especially if they do not have a certain title in life.

To be set free from this wrong thinking, one must surrender these feelings of failure to Jesus and trust in the fact that He will never leave or forsake you. He will be there to pick you up strengthen you, help you finish the plan he has for your future. Remember that God doesn't always call people to task who are qualified, He qualifies you along the way. Hebrews. 3:1

God is not interested in your success or failure, He is interested in you!

God Qualifies you to the Task
He has called you—

Trust

Leaders, generally speaking have limited trust. Like me, you probably had your share of disappointments, failures and losses, some of which was self-impose because of risk-taking and greed. I was a risk-taker; most business people are. I took foolish money risk with the get rich schemes and it cost a lot of heart sorrow. I also took risks in stocks and company organizations just to be accepted.

Again, God stepped in to save me, but not in the way I wanted. He saved me in the way that I needed. I was greedy and wanted to save my business for me, but God wanted to save my life, so He shut it down. I believe God directed me to write this book to deliver you from the greed of success. God is calling you to help people and you can't help them if you don't have the helper in your life.

Fear

The Lord did not give me a spirit of fear, but power, love and a sound mind. 11 Timothy 1:7.

Sometimes we are placed in a circle of circumstances that causes us feel powerless and out of control. Oftentimes, we give our power away and feel helpless. This should not be the case, especially for leaders. When you are in Christ, he gives you power for every situation. His anointing raises you higher than your circumstances. When you put your hope and assurance in the word of an unshakable and unmovable God, you can't help but win. God will give you childlike faith. Faith is the substance of things hoped for and the evidence of things not seen. Hebrews 11:1

Remember, God loves you and me so much that when we trust in Him, it becomes incorruptible seed that brings forth a good harvest. You get love, peace, healing, kindness and so much more. 1 Peter 1:23.

I am a testimony that God not only turned my life around, He saved my entire family. He can do the same for you. One important thing I learned from God as I grew my business and He grew me is that you cannot pull him out for emergencies only when you think you need help. He has to b Lord over all of your life. When you abide in

Christ and He abides in you, you live to God and he lives through you.I have found this journey to be worth waking up to see what he has in store for another day.

Money and Influence

As a Godly business owner God showed me the value and purpose of money .In Malachi 3:8 Because of God's unmerited favor, I learned to depend on Him as my source. It took me a long time to come to that understanding because just like all other parts of my life I had to learn his purpose. Over the years I have been business, God Has done a lot of things by his grace that I know would have taken me years. I applied the principles of tithe with 10% of my income and things worke out past my experiences. When people were looking for employees God kept my staff full I continued to see his hand in my favor by keeping my salon full of workers while other salons were looking for workers. He kept paying my bills even when I did not have clients. I believe it was because I was applying the principles that he is responsible to direct my life. I was sowing seed where I needed a harvest. As I continued growing in the Lord, I came to understand that tithing is not a law, but it is a Honor. Of course, we have a choice; therefore you should always tithe from your heart.

The gold is mine, The silver is mine, I allow you to use it to be my resource. 1 King 20:3

The Lord asks for all or nothing, and for your all, He will give you the desires of your heart. Psalms 37:4 He gave me back so much more than I could ever imagine. He will do the same for you because He loves you as much as He loves me. However, He wants to know who has your heart. Is it Him or is it money? Trust in Him and give out of obedience. Tithe ten percent of your gross income and He will not fail you.

2

<u>LIGHT ON A HILL</u>

God said he will give you the desire of your heart and it always line up with his will.

This is when God released me from people bondage and selfish ambitions. I no longer cared what people thought nor was I going to go backward especially after he had brought me so far spiritually. God said I will never leave you or forsake you. Hebrew 13:5 I believe Him.

God says come to me all who are heavy laden and I will give you rest. Matthew. 11:28

In order to become the new you, the old you must be left behind. This is the transformation process, and we are transformed by the renewing of our mind. Romans 12:2 Your thinking has to change so that you can agree with the word of God.

Grace to Transformation

The definition of transformation: To alter the state of form to another. In our case we are receiving our original nature back.

Step 1 : Know who you are. You are a three part being – you are a spirit living in a fleshy body that has a mind.

Step 2: Resist temptation with God's word. Walk in victory; walk in the spirit and do not fulfill the lust of the flesh.

Step 3: Faith without works is dead. You need faith with corresponding action. All of us has been given a measure of faith. When you get up in the morning, do you believe your legs with hold you up? Furthermore, do you believe that when you lie down, you will get up in the morning? Of course you do because last night when you were on the phone, you told people "see you later." That's faith. So why not put it to greater use by having faith in God!!

Step 4: Start Living. The just live by faith Habakkuk 2:4 When you understand who you are and whose you are, it becomes easier to understand the difference between greed and true wealth. Greed is to want more than one can afford at the time.. Wealth is being whole in all areas of life – family, business,, health, money, and your livelihood. We are not just consumers; we are God's problem solvers. God has divinely purposed a gift or talent within us all to fulfill while we are here on earth.

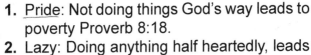

not just consumers but problem solvers

Product of Greed

1. Pride: Not doing things God's way leads to poverty Proverb 8:18.
2. Lazy: Doing anything half heartedly, leads to poverty
3. Foolish: Drunk and wasteful. Having Emotional reaction to situations without thinking. Proverb 29:11
4. Love of Money: We are to love God not His resources. Money is a resource. We are not to let money rule us. 1Timothy 6:10
5. Selfish: Anyone who doesn't give will be poor. Matthew 13:37
6. Hidden Sins: He who hides sin, his poverty will find him. 1John 1:9

You can never prosper past your place of knowing your strength and your weakness. Most of the time, we want to get out of where we are because we don't think it's fair. So we do what we want instead of asking God or doing what He has given us to do. The Bible tells us to acknowledge Him in all our ways and He will direct our paths. You may not be excited about where you are in your life, but this can be the very time to know that god has you right where he wants you and he has all the answers you need. It is the only way to a promotion in your life.

Where are you in your circle of influences

In my circle of influence I have spiritual mentors and teachers. He wanted me to be an example to other people whom he has placed in my life. My family,friends and my business. He has given me. I became a example to them by sharing the grace of Jesus. They both received Christ in their lives. Because I was faithful with those gifts, the doors opened for other business ventures areas including teaching, counseling and mentoring. I am constantly thanking God for business and people that he has placed in my life to share his grace to.

3

ANOINTED

I used to think that preachers were the only ones who were anointing from God. Many of you can breathe easier because that isn't true. It was a lack of knowledge on my part.11 Corinthian1-21 When you seek God, He will always lead you to the truth because He is the creator. He understands us. Therefore, through faith, you can have a relationship with god through Jesus. I remember my first experience of how much god loves me .I attended a class in my church which helped me understand the bible, One of the members in the church recommended I take the class called Bible One on One. However, the class was not a class about the Bible; it was a class on how you saw yourself in God's eyes. Through this class, I realized that I was angry and did not know who I was in Christ.

I was walking in wrong understanding trying to please God with works.

During one class, the question was asked, "How do you know you are ? Ephesians 2:5-8, Also Rom 10:9 If you confess with your mouth and believe in your heart that Jesus died for your sins and rose from the dead you are saved. The next question was "Then why aren't you walking in who God says you are and prospering in all areas of your life. This is when my healing started... when I read, "unless you receive His love, you aren't healed."

After taking this class, I knew how much God love me not based on my right and wrong. Take a moment and read Psalms 51 and receive His love now!

The reason this is such a great thing to know is that all you need is based on God love and not humanity definition of love. This love of life is conditional. God love is unconditional. Jeremiah 31- 1 It was also at that time that I discovered that this was the answer for me to have productive relationship with many people that I have encountered . I honor the call to pass on wisdom to those who do not understand. The grace from God is for edifying the saints and learning to walk as one .We must spend time with God and his word. How can you hear unless you hear a preacher. 1 Timothy 2:7 Gifting without understanding leads to confusion.

When leaders walk in their true identify which is in Christ, there is no competition or lack of

34

confidence. If I did not step out in my gifts, you would not be reading this book. So, let God lead you to your gifts so you can empower the next generation.

Godly Gift of Service: You love to help others

Godly Gift of Teaching: It is easy for you to pass down to others what you learn

Godly Gift or Encouragement: You motivate and inspire others

Godly Contribute to the needs of others: You are blessed to bless others in their need

Godly Leadership skills: You are a natural manager who can easily serve people and situations

Godly Mercy: You have a heart that feels the pain of others, forgiveness and compassion is a part of you.

These are the unconditional gifts from God 1 Tim 4:4.

4

GODLY LEADERSHIP

The walk of life is not easy, but we should always remember to stay focused on the "High Call." The focus is always bigger than us. Distractions will always be around John 16:23. For instance, just as I started writing this book, I received a call from my doctor who wanted me to come in for an exam. He wanted to make sure there were no cancer cells In my body. I immediately thank god for healing me and continue to focus on my faith in God. Yes, I am cancer free today because God healed me of cancer! This short interruption I thank god I Had Godly wisdom and friends and family to be by my side.

Why is faith so important? It shows obedience to a vision even when all goes against you. Your purpose is your vision that God gave you to fulfill through your gifts. Your purpose is to help others find their way through you and godly wisdom.

Your purpose is your vision that God gave you to fulfill through the use your gifts. How you perceive your purpose and gifts is critical. Let your perception always strive to see it God's way. You should always be in communication with God and make it a habit to ask Him how to handle situations.

For example: Imagine you are a business owner and one of your employees is a troublemaker. Is your first reaction to fire the employee? No! In this situation the employee may have children and a family or is a single parent who really needs the job. These were just a few situations I encountered in my business. I prayed and asked God what to do. God revealed to me that this employee wanted to be a leader. So I began to ask for this employee's input on programs and new ventures. Her entire attitude changed. If I would have obeyed my natural perceptions, instead of being in tune with God, I may have fired the young lady, but I want to operate in excellence – in the spirit. Gal 3:25

The Purpose of Honor

Honor starts first with God, the creator of the universe. Honoring God opens the door to honoring others. When you honor the people God have priority in order and in your life, God, family, Ministry, work entertainment Honor your wife or husband. Honor is always uplifting. "Those who honor me, I will honor. 1 Samuel 12:30

37

Covenant Relationships

We should choose covenant relationships instead of relationships based on temporary positions.1 Corinthians 6) 14

Abraham was in covenant with God. Genesis15: 18. It was a relationship based on trust and honor. Covenant relationships remind you of the participation and the commitment of both parties. The big vision of covenant relationship is always "Seek the kingdom of God and His righteousness and all things shall be added to you. Luke 12: 31.

You should make sure the person you are in covenant with supports what God placed inside of you. For instance, if you are trying to save, you don't need to be in covenant with someone who is always pulling you to spend. Givers should make sure they do not go into covenant with takers. Givers always bring in the productivity.

In the Bible, Joseph had dream (vision from God). He held on to his dreams through trials and tribulations. He was talked about and lied on. He was abandoned by the friends he had helped. But he knew God's words are true and never let go of his integrity. He did what was right even when no one was looking.

In my life in the marketplace, I have witnessed many people compromise values to get what they want on jobs by cheating or treating someone unfairly. The Bible tells us that the Lord adds wealth and adds no sorrow. Proverb:10,22

This is the reason many businesses are not successful.

When I was learning my relationship were about integrity, I would complain to God about how unfair everyone was and then I wondered why things didn't get better. Why wasn't God doing something? Then one day as I read the word of God, I had to examine what was holding up the process. I examined myself according to the word of God. He told me to acknowledge Him in all my ways, and He would direct my paths. I realized I had not been quiet to listen to God because I was trying to do things my way. This time I was listening and He led me to The Lord's Prayer.

Our Father, who is in heaven; hollow be thy name,
Thy kingdom come, His will be done on earth as it is in heaven
Give us this day; our daily bread
Forgive us our debts, as we forgive our debtors
Lead us not into temptation, but deliver us from evil
For His is the kingdom, the power and the glory
Forever and ever Amen

What I need to do was forgive and pray for the very people I was complaining about. This was not what I expected to hear or wanted to do, but it is the best way God's way.

Purpose for things beyond Me

5

THE CALLING

Ask yourself this question, Who are you leading or serving, Who are you leaving a heritage for. When we come the end of ourselves, we realize that we are n are created beings. When we accept Jesus as our savior, our priorities begin to line up and order comes to our lives.

In the early days of my business, my priorities were partially in order and I didn't realize I was compromising my best potential. In my drive to succeed, I put many things before God, and of course, it did not bring peace, all these thing are temporal we are to seek the things that are Eternal. Proverb 2-21. As I came to the end of myself, I received real peace and joy and purpose for things beyond me.

I also learned that we are not a product of a situation, but situations are subject to us. *God*

supplies all our needs according to his riches and glory. Philippians 4:19.

In the beginning of opening a business, You will encountered many lifestyles and personalities. In all those situations, You have the opportunity to bring honor to God. We always have a choice how to manage problems. For instance business turn for the worse and you don't know what to do and you have run out of all natural ideas. This has happen to me many times. One time I had a time when clients were affected by the downturn of lay-offs and my rent was due. I am glad that I have a covenant with god cause this was a serious situation and I needed peace fast!! I remember that God ways aren't like ours and once I Acknowledge the lord in all your ways and he shall direct your path Proverb 3: I. I prayed about the situation and the answer was whatever a man sow into the work of the gospel and you will reap a harvest Galatians 6:7. Trusting God is always a reward. Later not only did I get a payment plan to pay as I like, but I also was given a chance to close out my lease 6 months early with no break of contract fees. This was great a lot of stress was taken off of me and family. My point is God does not want us to worry about anything no matter what. He is a covenant keeper .God takes our cares off us so we will not have to .We are all in covenant with God to work on our behalf because of his grace toward us, through our relationship with Jesus and trust in the love of God .*He shall supply all my needs according*

Learning to Trust God (handwritten)

problems (handwritten)

WHY? (handwritten)

TRUST (handwritten)

to His riches in glory by Christ Jesus. Philippians 4:-19.. Cast all your cares on me because I care for you". I learned early to trust God in my affairs.

Obstacles are training opportunities valuable for maturing you for your destiny. Don't run away from problems, run toward them. As a leader, always recheck your motives and why you want to do what you are trying to do.

Ask yourself: Why do you want to be married? Why do you want children? Why do you want a business? Why do you want a six-figure income? If the reasons are to become complete, it is the wrong motive. It is only in Christ that we are complete. What a great pleasure to do all that we do to the glory of our Father. Revelation 4:11.

Start where you are. If God called you, He will qualify you.

Do you believe that God is love and that He loves you and His love will never fail? The challenge is to live by faith and not by sight. God is dependable, trustworthy, true, proven, solid, loyal, steadfast and faithful.

Here is another example of another transition that happen 4 employees left at the same time. I was devastated and I felt alone. I came to the crossroads in my life that challenged my faith. I had to believe God's word over people and at the same see where I was in my faith. This was the hardest for me because just like any business owner you put a lot of time any money in what you do. I knew I had to go to my covenant in Jesus and get some real help. I needed my mind at peace and all the hurt to go away today!! I screamed lord this isn't fair. One thing I love about God he allows you to vent and he will not leave you or forsake you. Hebrew 13:5. As usual his way always he is always on time.. Later he did just that, and not only did he bring me out but my relationship has grown closer to him and I learned not to do anything without his direction. God tells us that I know the thoughts that I think toward you said, the lord Thoughts of peace, and not of evil, to give you an expected end Jeremiah 29:11. What a Faithful God we serve here we are 3 years later sharing his faithfulness to you. Also God has blessed me with a company that reach out to youth that are high-risk, and let they know they don't have to feel guilty about the decisions in the past, but to know that God has a plan for their life and they still can live out dreams that are in their hearts. Our Company has and will help changes lives from the inside out. By inspiring, teaching, and empowering. Our prayer is that through our inspiration and journey that this book has help you realize that you can dream again. Our goal is to direct you back to your God given dream and build you up to be a awesome youth, woman or man in the Marketplace, God Bless you and may you never let trials keep you from developing to be the successful person in Jesus Christ. Thank God for allowing me to walk through this journey with you as you continue to read on.

6

__BEST THREE YEARS__

There was a lot for me to learn about time as a leader. One thing we can all admit we don't control time. This bring me to the next thing that I am sure you have asked yourself what will I do with my precious time as a gift from God. Ephesians 5:16 We know that it is a gift cause we would love to change some of the things we did or did not do in our life time. The vision is the beginning of of purpose in our lives and it has its fulfillments that you learn along the way. The thing that Godly leaders have to remember that we don't just do the moral thing but the godly thing, ill go into a little more detail when I was in business for the first year. I had a particular worker and all were doing business well everything seemed ok. One day I drove to the salon early than usual. One of the workers was sleeping in her car outside the business with her children and not one of the workers or I had one idea how long she was outside . You may say this happens all the time,not so the first thing I thought was how can people work around you for so long and no one knows you or you don't even care to open up to your workers about help. This taught me that this was one area That as leaders it is our business and God has entrusted you with them as your employees . First lesson I learned is my prayer life increased. I ask God to give me wisdom to discern problems and issues to bring to prayer. 2Peter 1:7 . Once you do the will and allow God to enlarge your territory for the sake of lifting up people and letting them see Christ in you. I also learned that I never had to advertise for workers. Now I am not saying that its not good but god always has a better way when we just allow him to bring honor to your name. Gods wisdom will bring you places that may take others a long time and effort to receive .Proverb 4)8

The increase will always bring with it a new set of issues and as a leader God trust we will handle. One of the things a leader strongest thing to know that the opposite of the vision is people will want you to do things their way and you will be misunderstood.

As a leader your character will be tested and tried! There will be areas in your character that will be tested . God loves you and he will not bring any bad to you but the enemy does.

As we look at Joseph in the bible he was given a vision from God and he quickly wanted to brag about it and what did it cause him. The one thing we must remember like Joseph is that when God give you a vision and one of the thing he remembered is That the world that is out of Gods will don't understand spiritual things. Genesis 37:23

The Truth upholds everything 1 Timothy 3:15 . I can relate this to the dream Gave me and just like Joseph all will seem to come against it . I heard may words of doubt and especially wondered if I qualified to be all god had for me, but you hold on to what God word says about you . Along the way if you have diverse situations of money loss and friends lost Hold on to your dream . Gods Favor will follow you in your most challenging situations. During this walk you will be falsely accused or even get be betrayed but Gods favor will bring you through. Genesis 39:21.

I want to point out an important thing that what kept me through all hardships was remembering that God gave me a dream . This was God building his strength in me. Proverbs 18:16. This is a urgent need for people to never to let go of their dreams and I am here to encourage you to not let go!! I trusted in the unshakeable promise of God. This was a decision that I had to make no matter what I held on to the word of God. During this time of waiting God taught me to be a blessing to others.

I developed a right attitude which will always parallels your vision. In all things doing it the way God wants will always cause you to be better not bitter.

You will even come back across the same people that cross you and God will ask you to forgive and forget . He did it for me and you so he expects you to do the same.

This is when you learn that God Has given you everything in the inside and this is why I express to you that God has a plan in your life and He has a plan of good and not of evil,to bring you to a expected end.

Shaky Foundations

7

<u>YOU ARE MORE</u>

I thank God for his faithfulness to his covenant to us. This allows me to share to you the purpose of all this. I HAVE COME TO STAND ON A FOUNDATION THAT NEVER FAILS. There is no one who wants to rely or depend on a shaky foundation.

Think about it in a natural way when you purchase a home when you look you search all their credits and the builders history.

This is where the cross of Jesus Christ is in our life and his grace has never left us. God has loved us since the foundation of the earth. Jeremiah 31:3 . God has destined a purpose for me and you. There is not a single thing on earth that was made that is wasted all things were created for the glory of God pleasure. Psalm 149:4. Do we live at our lowest potential that has been given to us from experience or past.

This has been a question for many that I have come across. In beginning God made us in his likeness Genesis 1:26. All humanity is searching for identity, and all have yet to find a perfect one who they can understand them when we all need broken pieces to be healed. Our nature is to adapt to culture and social approval and job God has made us to live off of the substance of love. We look for it and we abuse it toss it around like it is a layaway plan. I hope I have your attention cause is not real love. Love according to God is John 3:16. God so loved the world that he gave his only begotten son that who believe him would have ever lasting life. This is the glory that god created us for and we will never experience true love or be able to share it without receiving Jesus. God say we have all fallen short of his glory. Do not live your life living up to standards that you will never measure. We have a loving father who will show you the way the truth and the light. John 14:6. God wants a relationship with us so we don't have to live in pain, hurt, sickness, fear, disappointments and failure. He sent his son to mend the brokenhearted give sight to the blind and set the oppressed free. Isaiah 58:6. I want to go back to the word love that we use so loosely. The word means to never run out unconditional. When we look at our life we have run out of love for many reasons and some of us don't even want to hear the word cause it has been a tool of deception for people to take advantage of a people that has been hurt and looking for true comfort. This separation from God has man searching for his entire life for the true love that can only come from his heavenly father. Romans 10:3. We have to return back to our creator through a sinless redeemer Jesus .He who knew no sin became sin for us so that we could be reconciled back to our father . Ephesians 2:16. The best investment you can make is in yourself and your eternity

SALAVATION PRAYER

Father you said in your word that if I come to you and repent of sins according to Romans 10:9 and believe in my heart that Jesus died on the cross for all my sins yesterday today and forever and rose back up for me (put you name) that you would forgive me and cleanse me of all unrighteous .

Father I thank you for loving me and I receive forgiveness today in Jesus name. Heavenly Father I thank you for filling me with the Holy Ghost. I receive your love to the fullest today in Jesus name. I thank you that all my Sins are washed away . Isaiah 1: 16. Heavenly father I thank you for wisdom, understanding and knowledge of you today in Jesus name. Amen

8

GRACE AND SUPPLY A BETTER WAY

Fight the good fight of faith, take hold of eternal life for which you were called when you made your good confession. 1Timothy 6:12

Welcome to the new journey of a life filled with value and purpose. Once I started this journey after confession and acceptance. I was ready to know why am I created and what do I do now. After all the hardships and relationships that failed I came to a place of running out of ideas and everyone you go to has problems they are trying to get answer to as well. As you embark this new journey of purpose this life is so easy to relate to when you were born out of your mother womb and as a baby you had to rely on a parent to teach you .This is the same thing that you have to do now that you are learning about the real you. You are a spirit. We are a spirit with a will that consist of emotions, intellect and desires. We live in flesh which is the house of gods Spirit. Our body is the temple of the living god. 11 Corinthians 6:16. People don't perish from who they are but what they don't know. God says in his word that perseverance must finish its work so that you may be mature and complete not lacking anything, and if any of you lack wisdom he should ask God. James 1:4.

Here I learned that this was going to be a challenge that God has my life already planned and now I have to trust him. Jeremiah 1:5. I know from walking with God that True leaders serve and the opposite of serving has always cause man to lose focus. Don't give up hope this may seem to be a bit overwhelming at first but just like when you were a baby you Had no effort to grow to where you are now. Jesus wants to develop you so that you will be equipped for your appointment for such a time as this. 11 Timothy 3:17

. I live my life to be a distinction that others want or strive to reach for God so they too can live on the same grace given from our loving father. Our lives are to have value and in order to accomplish that it will go beyond self and stuff.. God is the creator of us and he is so concerned about you and all he has put in your surroundings .I always say to people that one thing for sure you can't change is your race or what family you were born into. We are all flawed fallen from the grace of God. We live in a world that speaks of freedom and since we all crave it and the reason so is it came from God. The true definition is The lord is spirit and where the spirit of the lord is freedom. 11 Corinthians 3:17. When a baby is growing they are going through a stage of its all about me and my way. I remember that stage as a baby christian and I didn't understand why I could not have things my way and when things didn't work I would say something is wrong with others. Remember this is how we have to grow into our relationship with God and when you find out that he will speak directly to you about you.

This is the time that I had to dig into the word of god and learn of him for myself. He promises that those who seek after me will be filled Psalm 107:9. The Most important

Journey is that God will show you is that he loves you unconditional, and that he want to shower his love in you to others that are in your life. This is the challenge that I had because running was my favorite way to get out of things. I understand why God tells us to not to forsake the assembly of the church of God. I strongly speak on the teaching of Jesus Christ. Romans 10:14 I ask the lord to guide me to a church that I can receive teaching.

This was the precious stage in my life like so many new babies, I have never seen a baby that someone heart that didn't get touched by . This is why I never will forget my first experience in coming back to Jesus. Our natural parents will show pictures of the same baby even when they are grown and married. God did the same thing to me when I kept settling for below average living. He kept pulling on my heart with love and concern. I rejoiced that my father love me just as I was and now it was time to grow up . You know like I know being a baby means I don't have to be responsible. I did know that either I stay a loner or get this relationship thing right. God created relationships to develop us Genesis 2:18 . Now that I have this new life it should bring honor to my father and bring all around me to his grace. If you are married or single or desire to be married or if you are in the state I was in a marriage that had a title but no real substance. The answer is the order that god made before we seek to be bosses or leaders in the workforce developing our relationship will determine if you will grow from the baby stage or become respon- sible. Let us not love with words and tongue, but with action and in truth. 1John 3:18 I had decided that I only wanted what was the best and tried it Gods way and have peace in my home and life. I remember that I wanted to be a distinction that people will follow and a spirit of reconciliation is a mark of a christian. Relationships are important to God and how we respond to people and treat them . God so loved the world that he gave his only begotten son .John 3:16. As you continue to draw close to the relationship with god through reading the bible, attending church and keeping like minded people around you .The goal of reaching a champion will be the mark that will not be forgotten. This was the start of great things to come and there is a order that has already been established for us to fulfill this journey. I quickly learned that the order is relationship with God, then family then church then the community we live in. I myself realized that I had to alter my life-style. The first time it was very challenging and I had made up my mind that freedom does come with a price and that price was to do it Gods way and what a great reward .So at this stage of your life you will have to decide and there will be no fans to push you or groups to motivate you this is a personal decision with you and God. I can assure you that you will not be put to shame or disappointed. Psalm 34:8.

9

<u>BELIEVE</u>

This race is not for the swift or the battle to the strong, nor does food come to the wise or wealth to the brilliant or favor to the learned : but time and chance happen to them all.

You decide that you are created to be a champion because of the word of your father.

This challenge is not for the faint or popular or crowd pleaser but for followers of Jesus.

These are the steps that you will have to experience to be solid and unmovable in your in faith. We discussed freedom and its price. The next challenge is excellence and being a doer no matter what. Remember I said this was a challenge and greater is he that is in you than he that is in the world. Jesus said that he will never leave you or forsake you.

Trusting

Bitter 2 Better